YOUNG PEOPLE'S STORY OF
OUR HERITAGE

YOUNG PEOPLE'S
STORY OF
OUR HERITAGE

AFRICA AND ASIA

by

V. M. HILLYER and E. G. HUEY

New Edition Designed and Revised by Childrens Press, Chicago

Consultants

William T. Nichol, Principal
Charles Gates Dawes Elementary School, Evanston, Illinois

John R. Lee, Professor of Education
Northwestern University, Evanston, Illinois

Meredith Press, New York

Illustrations in the order in which they appear

Library of Congress Catalog Card Number: 66-11335

Copyright © 1966 by Meredith Publishing Company. Originally published under the title of *A Child's Geography of the World* by V. M. Hillyer. Revised and Enlarged Edition, with new material by Edward G. Huey. Copyright, 1929, by The Century Co. Copyright, 1951, by Appleton-Century-Crofts, Inc. Copyright, 1957, by Mercantile Safe Deposit and Trust Co. All rights reserved. Printed in the U.S.A. Published simultaneously in Canada.

Contents

Acknowledgments

Cover, top: An Oriental boat called a sampan
John Hollis—Hollis Associates

Cover, bottom: Bengal tiger, India
John Hollis—Hollis Associates

Page 2: The Mohammed Aly Citadel, Egypt
Egyptian State Tourist Administration. Photo by
C. Zachary.

Frontis: A Buddhist monument called a Dagoba, Ceylon
American President Lines

Opposite: High waves of Lake Tanganyika menace the
native thatched hut near the shore at Albertville, Congo
United Nations

Designer: Marita Kling

Project Editor: Joan Downing

Manuscript Editor: Margaret Friskey

Editorial Staff: Frances Dyra,
  Mary Reidy, Gerri Stoller

AFRICA AND ASIA

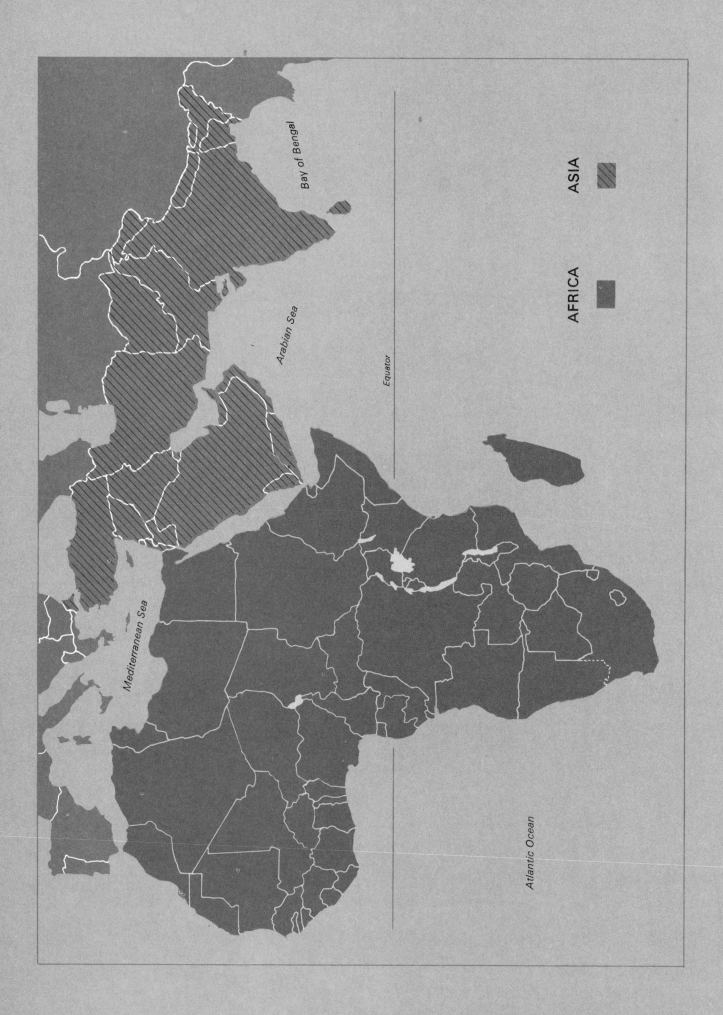

Bay of Bengal

Arabian Sea

Mediterranean Sea

Equator

Atlantic Ocean

ASIA

AFRICA

Introduction

Africa and Asia—Asia and Africa. What stories seem to hide behind these names! And most of us have learned what we know about them from stories. These stories told just a bit of what life was like at a certain time and in a certain place. Most of the stories were written by Europeans, and the peoples of Africa and Asia were seen through European eyes.

Today we want to know how Africa and Asia seem to the African and the Asian. We want to know how the Malayans feel about Malaysia, and the Congolese about the Congo. For one important fact about the world today is that so many of the nations in Africa and Asia are new. In Africa alone, twenty-seven countries became free between 1960 and 1966. Free here means free of rule by Europeans—free to decide what sort of government they want and what sort of life they want. Free is a magical word to all of us, and particularly to people who have been ruled for hundreds of years by others.

Africa and Asia are both huge continents. The people, and language, and customs are very different from place to place. About the only thing most of the people have in common is a determination to stay free. This determination is changing Africa and Asia. So come on a magic journey and see what the countries and the peoples of Africa and Asia are like today.

opposite: The Continents of Africa and Asia

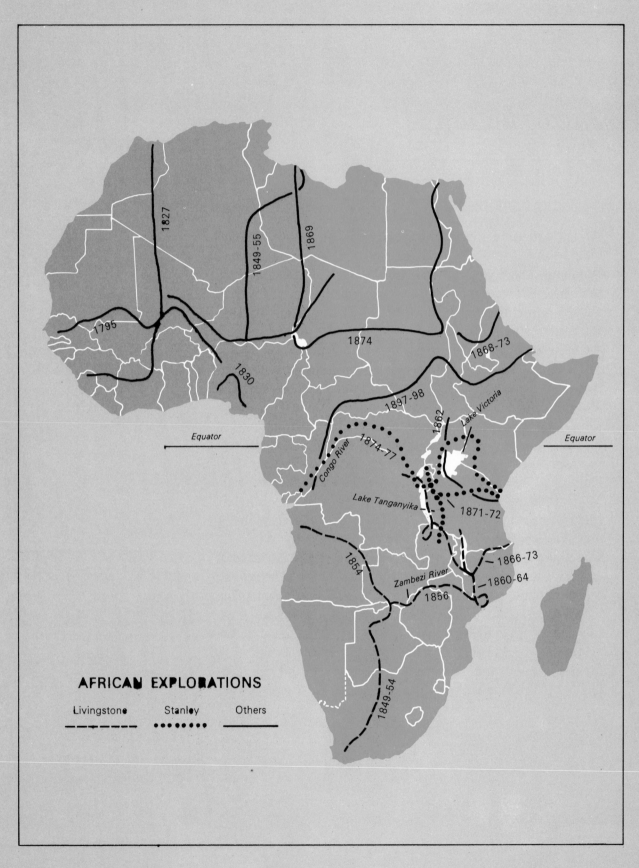

1827

1849-55

1869

1795

1830

1874

1868-73

1897-98

1862

Lake Victoria

Congo River

1874-77

Lake Tanganyika

1871-72

1854

1866-73

Zambezi River

1860-64

1856

1849-54

AFRICAN EXPLORATIONS

Livingstone   Stanley   Others

Equator   Equator

12

Africa, the Waking Giant

Next to Asia, Africa is the biggest continent of the earth.

You may once have thought of Africa as the home of the crocodile in the Limpopo River. Or of the camel on the desert. Or as the place that the giraffes and hippos in the zoo came from.

Many delightful tales and strange animals have come from Africa. But these are just the beginning of Africa's wonderful story. Much of its story has been written in the last hundred years—even in the last ten.

It is true that long before the time of Christ the northern coast of Africa was settled. Cities along the Mediterranean Sea traded with Europe and with Greece.

Arab traders sailed along the east coast of Africa. They were looking for slaves and ivory.

Early European sailors followed the west coast of Africa to get down to and around this continent. It stood in the way of getting to the "Spice Islands" near India. If these sailors stopped at the Cape of Good Hope as they rounded Africa, it was to get fresh food and water.

The Dutch were the first to stop at the Cape of Good Hope and start a colony. This was sixty-five years after the Pilgrims landed at Plymouth in the New World.

There were good reasons why early settlers and explorers did not go far beyond the coast of Africa. If they didn't run into a desert, they ran into a jungle. If they went up a river, a waterfall stopped them.

For hundreds of years little was known about Africa. It was called the "Dark Continent."

Much of Africa is like a dented frypan turned upside down. It is a series of high, rolling tablelands called *plateaus*. These end abruptly near the sea. Rivers plunge off the plateaus in wildly beautiful falls and rapids.

The equator (ee-kway'tore) runs through Africa. Parts of the west coast, the Congo Basin, and the east coast are hot and humid. The high plateaus give most of Africa a pleasant climate. Half the continent is grassland. Desert areas, of course, are hot and dry.

There are no great mountain ranges in Africa as there are on other continents. However, one of the earth's biggest cracks runs through this land. It is called the "African Rift Valley." A rift valley is formed when the land sinks between two faults (places where the bedrock can shift). The high plateaus in east Africa are broken by this rift valley. It is over a hundred miles wide. It begins in Syria (sear'ee-ah) and Israel (iz'ree-uhl). It includes the Red Sea. It runs through east Africa to Lake Nyasa (nye-ass'ah).

Africa has nearly every kind of land and climate.

There are flat grasslands called the *veld*.

There are dim, steaming rain forests. The trees grow so high and thick that sunlight may never reach the ground.

There are hot, dry deserts. The Sahara (suh-hair'ah) is as big as the continental United States.

Low coastal plains ring the continent. Rivers fall to them from the plateaus and drop African mud into the sea.

There are river valleys and a few mountains.

Parts of Africa get almost no rain. Parts get too much.

There are as many ways of living in Africa as there are kinds of land. It is the people who make the story of a continent.

Africans may live in a modern city or in a grass hut. They may live in a palace or a nomad's tent. They may fly to work or ride in a dugout canoe. They may dance to modern jazz or to a jungle tom-tom.

Past and present are often side by side as the people of Africa look toward an exciting future.

opposite top: Aerial view of Durban, South Africa

opposite bottom: Couple walking along a new highway in Swaziland

South African Information Service

John Moss of Black Star for IDA

Light in the
Dark Continent—
South Africa

A little more than a hundred years ago, a Scot named Dr. David Livingstone went exploring the unmapped heart of Africa. He started from Port Elizabeth at the very southern tip of the continent.

He traveled by oxcart across the Kalahari Desert. West of the Kalahari, the Namib Desert is too dry for any life. But the Kalahari with its hot white sands had some grass and brush. Bushmen lived here and hunted the wild game.

Dr. Livingstone went more than five hundred miles into the continent. He walked through high grass and traveled on rivers whenever he could. He waded through swamps and became sick with fever. A wounded lion attacked him and an elephant charged at him. Though Livingstone went as a missionary, he made all-important maps. He wrote glowing letters about the beauty of the country.

On other trips he went into Africa from the west coast and in from Zanzibar on the east coast. He once followed the Zambesi (zam-bee'zee) River into the continent and discovered the greatest waterfall in the world—twice as high as Niagara Falls and half again as wide! He heard the roar of these falls when he was twenty miles away. The natives called them the falls of "sounding mist." Livingstone named them after Victoria, who was then the Queen of England.

You remember we said that the Dutch first settled the southern part of Africa where Dr. Livingstone began his journey. Much has happened since the time those first Dutch settlers came to South Africa. The British came and clashed with the descendants of the Dutch, called

opposite: Zulu woman in colorful tribal dress

Boers. The Boers left the area and made the "Great Trek" northward to the High Veld where they set up the Boer Republic with the provinces called the Orange Free State, between the Orange and Vaal rivers, and the Transvaal, between the Vaal and Limpopo rivers. When you sing "We are marching to Pretoria," you are singing about the Great Trek, for Pretoria is in the Transvaal. In fact, Pretoria is now the capital of the Republic of South Africa.

The Boers and British eventually went to war. The British won and the two white groups were united, though there is still disagreement between the two groups. The English-speaking descendants of the British are sometimes called Europeans; the Boers, now called *Afrikaners*, speak *Afrikaans*, a language that is a mixture of Dutch and some African words.

The Europeans tend to be more liberal in racial matters. The Afrikaners believe very strongly in the separation of the races, called *apartheid* (ah-pahr'tate). When the British Commonwealth of Nations spoke out against apartheid in 1964, the Republic, which is dominated by the Afrikaners, withdrew from the Commonwealth.

It is hard for anyone not living in Africa to realize how completely apartheid rules the lives of both the whites and the natives in South Africa. By laws passed from 1948 on, the white population and the other races have almost nothing to do with one another. Although the Bantus, as the whites call the natives, can work for Afrikaners and Europeans, either as servants or in mines or factories, they cannot have homes in white areas. Certain sections of the Republic have been set aside as Bantu areas, and this is the only place the natives have rights and can own homes. The white areas are much larger and more fertile than the scattered Bantu areas. When Bantu men come into the white areas to work, they must leave their families in the Bantu areas.

opposite: A rural Bantu school in Pretoria, South Africa. The word and picture charts on the walls show the two official languages of the republic—English and Afrikaans.

The Republic of South Africa today is probably the most modern of all the African countries, but the growth of apartheid has also made it the unhappiest and the most isolated.

The Union of South Africa is one of two African countries where a small group of white people still rule the many natives. (Rhodesia is the other.)

South African Information Service

Africa is a continent of many, many countries. While the Dutch and the British were opening South Africa, other European countries were dividing up the rest of the continent into territories.

As late as 1953 there were only four independent countries in Africa. They were Egypt, Liberia, Ethiopia, and Libya. Between 1960 and 1966, twenty-seven more became free of European control.

South West Africa was settled by Germans. It is now governed by the Republic of South Africa. It is a huge country, but not many people live there, for much of the country is the Namib Desert, which is too hot and dry to support life. Diamonds, however, are being mined there now.

You can still follow Livingstone's path into Africa from the south, but you now can leave a beautiful resort town on the southern seacoast by train, plane, helicopter, or automobile.

The land itself has not changed. Distances are great. There are deserts to cross and jungles to cut through. The land rises in steps to the High Veld.

The Kalahari Desert is still the home of the Bushmen, who support themselves on wild game. These small, slender people have yellow-brown skin and slightly slanted eyes. At one time, the Bushmen roamed all over southern Africa, but they were pushed north as the Bantu peoples came south. Bushmen artists painted pictures on rock walls over much of southern Africa. Much of the Bushmen's life and history has been learned from these fine pictures.

In the lowlands you can see grass huts that are built to shed the heavy rains.

You can see modern cities in the High Veld where skyscrapers reach glass fingers toward the sky and where modern airports are within a few hours of any part of the world.

Modern Johannesburg, in the Transvaal, is 6000 feet above sea level, so the climate is pleasant.

The people have made, and are continuing to make, the changes in South Africa. People are using the resources of the country. They are farming the fertile areas of the High Veld and grazing cattle in the drier areas of the north and west.

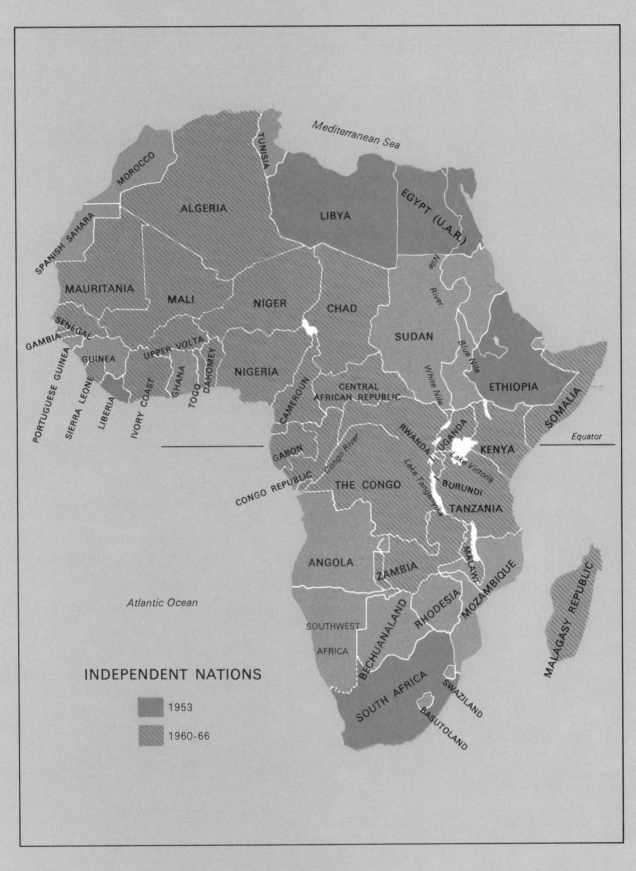

TUNISIA

Mediterranean Sea

MOROCCO

ALGERIA

LIBYA

EGYPT (U.A.R.)

SPANISH SAHARA

Nile River

MAURITANIA

MALI

NIGER

CHAD

SUDAN

SENEGAL

Blue Nile

GAMBIA

UPPER VOLTA

ETHIOPIA

PORTUGUESE GUINEA

GUINEA

DAHOMEY

NIGERIA

White Nile

SIERRA LEONE

GHANA

TOGO

CENTRAL AFRICAN REPUBLIC

SOMALIA

LIBERIA

IVORY COAST

CAMEROUN

RWANDA

UGANDA

KENYA

Equator

GABON

Congo River

Lake Victoria

CONGO REPUBLIC

THE CONGO

Lake Tanganyika

BURUNDI

TANZANIA

ANGOLA

ZAMBIA

MALAWI

Atlantic Ocean

MOZAMBIQUE

SOUTHWEST

BECHUANALAND

RHODESIA

MALAGASY REPUBLIC

AFRICA

SWAZILAND

SOUTH AFRICA

BASUTOLAND

INDEPENDENT NATIONS

1953

1960-66

The richest mineral belt in the world runs from Katanga Province in the Congo to the northern part of the Republic of South Africa. Much of the gold of the world comes from this area, as do most of the diamonds.

Africans are flown in from far and wide to work in the mines. They live in special villages at the mines and stay for as long as fourteen months before they are flown back to their families.

The force of falling water in the rivers is being used to generate electricity.

Bechuanaland (betsh-wahn'ah-land), in the center of South Africa, is one of three British High Commission Territories. It has been governed by a British Resident Commissioner, but will gain independence in 1966. Much of the Kalahari Desert is in this country. Some cattle hides, asbestos, gold, and manganese are exported. Many of the Africans of this country spend much of the year working in mines in the Republic.

Basutoland (bah-soo'toe-land), the second High Commission Territory, is much smaller than Bechuanaland, but has twice as many people. Most of the country is mountainous, and nearly all the people live in the western lowlands. They wear woolen clothing woven in gay patterns. Labor for the mines is about the only export. This country is ruled by a Resident Commissioner.

Swaziland (swahz'ee-land), on the east coast, is nearly surrounded by the Republic of South Africa. It is much smaller than either of the other High Commission Territories. Swaziland also is governed by a Resident Com-

above: Street in old section of Tananarive, Malagasy Republic

right: Moonlit lake in the Malagasy Republic

missioner. The soil is fertile and sugar, butter, and meat are exported, although asbestos is the most important export.

The Malagasy (mahl-ah-gass'ee) Republic is a large island. It is 200 miles off the coast of southeast Africa and once was known as Madagascar (mad-ah-gass'car). It became independent of France in 1960, but has remained a member of the French Community of Nations, which is much like the British Commonwealth of Nations. Coffee, sugar and vanilla are raised on this mountainous island.

If you follow the Zambesi River or the Limpopo from the east coast of southern Africa, you will go through Mozambique (moe-zahm-beek'), a Portuguese overseas province.

Across the continent on the Atlantic there is another Portuguese province, Angola (ahng-go'lah). Portuguese families were given a house, seeds, livestock, and 100 acres of land to go and live in Angola. Angola is fourteen times bigger than Portugal itself, but it is still sparsely settled.

below: Construction worker prepares blasting charge for a dam being built in Swaziland

Rhodesia, Zambia, and Malawi

If you keep following the river across Mozambique, you will come at last to Rhodesia.

If you had come this way in colonial days you would have found three countries—Southern Rhodesia, Northern Rhodesia, and Nyasaland.

In 1953 the three countries joined forces in a federation. It seemed a good idea at the time, but it didn't work out. Northern Rhodesia and Nyasaland had British governors, but most of the people were Negro Africans.

In Southern Rhodesia the small European minority had been granted self-government in 1923. Even now the European population is only seven per cent of the total. But many of these "Europeans" came from the Republic of South Africa. They brought the idea of apartheid with them.

When the federation of the three countries broke up, Nyasaland became the independent nation of Malawi (mah-lah'wee). Northern Rhodesia became the independent nation of Zambia. Rhodesia (formerly Southern Rhodesia) continued to be a British colony. But in October of 1965 it declared its independence from Great Britain. This declaration was made by the small white group. They wanted to continue to govern the country without giving representation to the large native African population. Great Britain did not accept this declaration of independence and stopped all trade with Rhodesia. Many other countries did, too.

Rhodesia has a Low Veld, a High Veld, and a Middle Veld.

The areas around the Zambesi River on the north and the Limpopo in the south are Low Veld. They are damp, unhealthy places with much malaria and sleeping sickness.

Most of the High Veld, where the rich mineral deposits are, is owned by Europeans.

The Middle Veld is suitable for farming, and most of it is owned by the native Africans. There is not enough land for all those who want to farm, so many of the natives drift to the cities. They get jobs but are paid less than Europeans doing the same work.

Most of the industry of Rhodesia is in the capital city of Salisbury.

Zambia is largely high plateau, between the Congo and the Zambesi rivers. Because it is high land, it is not so hot and humid as the Congo.

European settlers in Zambia live either in the north, near Tanganyika (tan-gahn-yee'kah), or near Malawi.

The copper belt of Zambia is a continuation of the mineral belt that runs through Katanga in the Congo. Over half the Africans who work in Zambia work in or around the mines. Some peanuts and tobacco are exported from Zambia, but most of the farming is done to feed the mine workers.

Malawi is the poorest of the three former federation countries. The low land around the Shire River and Lake Nyasa is hot and unhealthy. Most of the people live in the southern highlands.

Some farming is done. But the most important export is labor. Many of the men work in mining areas.

below: Copper-mine workers in Zambia happily return home

United Nations

26

The Congo

On one of his trips, as we mentioned, David Livingstone went into the heart of darkest Africa from the west coast. If you traveled in his footsteps down the Congo River in the west, you could see the brown mud dumped in the Atlantic long before you reached the mouth of the river.

The Congo is a long river. It flows through Africa for almost three thousand miles. But it is not all a peaceful waterway.

Like many other African rivers it falls toward the sea in a riot of rapids. You cannot ride up the river. But neither do you have to trek through miles of jungle to get around the rapids. A railroad now runs from Pointe-Noire (pwant-nah-wahr') on the Atlantic to Brazzaville. In its 320 miles it goes through twelve tunnels and crosses ninety-two bridges. Now much freight comes from the upper reaches of the river by rail around the rapids.

Brazzaville is the capital of the small Congo Republic. This was once a French colony. It gained a peaceful independence in 1958. Almost seventy-five per cent of the school-age children here go to school. It is particularly unusual that about one-third of these are girls, who do not generally get an education in tropical Africa.

In the Congo Republic trained elephants pull down trees and haul logs to the sawmills. Pineapples, citrus fruit, peanuts, coffee, and cocoa are among the crops exported. Lead, tin, zinc, gold, and a few diamonds are mined.

Many times bigger than the Congo Republic is the country known now simply as the Congo. It was formerly the Belgian Congo.

This whole vast area of land was given to King Leopold II of Belgium in 1885. Europeans thought he would rule

opposite: Group of diggers work on a railroad extension in the Congo Republic

well and free the land of slavery. But Leopold ruled the Congo brutally for twenty-three years. Several million people died in the Congo during this time. Public opinion finally forced Leopold to turn over the government of the Congo to the country of Belgium. Murder of the people ended but the Africans were still forced to labor on the rubber plantations.

People were better fed, but education was not offered to them. Even so, new ideas crept in, and in 1960 the Congo became independent of Belgium.

At this time there were only fourteen college graduates in this country of more than fourteen million people. There were no native officers in the army and few had had any experience in government jobs.

The Congo has had many problems since 1960. Within two weeks of independence, Katanga Province with its wealth of minerals, seceded. Rival tribes fought with each other. Three years of bloodshed followed before Katanga came back into the country. Rebellions continue to break out.

Half of this vast country is tropical rain forest. The highest part of the country is in the east. Mount Ruwenzori (roo-wehn-zore'ee) is almost seventeen thousand feet above sea level. Lake Tanganyika is the largest of a series of lakes.

Leopoldville, the capital, is a city of broad avenues and tall buildings.

The Congo River carries freight toward the Atlantic. Minerals are the most important export. But barges of coffee, rubber, cotton, and palm products also wend their way down the river through the forests.

The river is the heart of life in the Congo. People use the river as a highway. Children swim in it. Women wash their clothes in it. Men fish in it with bamboo traps or spears.

In places, the river is home to crocodiles and hippos.

Old and New Civilizations— the West Coast

If you go on up the west coast of Africa, you will find some of the finest and oldest Negro civilizations . . . and new nations emerging.

Nigeria (nye-jeer'ee-ah) is one of the largest and most important countries in Africa. It has a population of over fifty-five million. Nigeria became independent in 1960, but remained a part of the British Commonwealth of Nations.

The city of Benin (beh-neen') was once the capital of the ancient kingdom of Benin. This was a flourishing country when Portuguese traders first visited West Africa hundreds of years ago. Benin was renowned for its sculpture and carvings in wood, ivory, and brass. Nigerian artists still produce beautiful works of art.

Lagos, the national capital, is a very old city, too. It is built on an island and is connected to the mainland by a bridge. It was once a center for slave trading and the area around it was known as the Slave Coast.

The most important crops of Nigeria are peanuts, cocoa, cotton, palm oil, and bananas. Nigeria is the second largest producer of crude oil in the British Commonwealth. Some tin, gold, and tungsten, as well as coal are mined.

The children of Nigeria go to school. Teachers are being trained. There are five universities, two medical schools and a law school.

The southwest, with its tropical jungle, gets 200 inches of rain each year. The dry far north runs into the Sahara Desert. People adapt their way of living to the kind of land that is their home.

Nigeria today shows that different African tribes can work together to create a country, and still keep much of their own tribal cultures.

Nigerian woman sits on railroad tracks. In the background are stacks of metal ties.

Workers pan rich diamond deposits into baskets in Sierra Leone

Nigerian children watch a carpenter at work

Gambia (gam'bee-ah) is a geographical joke. It is only a narrow 300-mile strip along the Gambia River. Great Britain seized it in 1817 to keep the French from getting the river. The Gambia is one of the few navigable rivers in West Africa.

Gambia is entirely surrounded by Senegal, a member of the French Community of Nations.

The people of Gambia live near the river. They depend on it for transportation and communication. Most of them are farmers and raise peanuts.

Every year thousands of "strange farmers" come from neighboring countries to grow peanuts. They are given land and houses to live in while they are farming and return to their homes after the harvest in November.

Sierra Leone (see-air'ah lee-own') was set up as a home for ex-slaves who had fought for the English in the American Revolution. Freetown was established in 1792. The oldest university in West Africa is at Freetown.

The descendants of these freed slaves call themselves Creoles (cree'ohlz). They have a tradition of education, and have stayed aloof from the Africans in the rest of the country.

The coast is hot and humid. Tropical diseases flourish. Sierra Leone was long known as the "White Man's Grave," but modern disease prevention is changing this.

Rice is the important crop. But when diamonds were found in the riverbeds, many farmers went to mining. Rice had to be imported. But people who were very poor now have a chance to prosper away from the villages.

Sierra Leone became independent in 1961. It is part of the British Commonwealth of Nations.

Liberia (lye-beer'ee-ah) was a poor land until 1945. At that time, with aid from the United States government and large firms like the Firestone Rubber Company, things began changing. Schools have been started and modern agriculture is improving the farms.

High-grade iron ore is mined in the north. Diamonds are mined by three companies and also by individuals.

In Liberia, unlike many African nations, any citizen with a pick and shovel can mine diamonds. Only people of African descent, however, can become citizens. And only citizens can own land there.

Other Western Countries

Ghana (gahn'ah) became the first Negro African republic within the British Commonwealth of Nations in 1960. Since then, she has played an important role in Africa.

Once this was called the Gold Coast, but as a new nation it took the name of Ghana. This had been the name of a wealthy African empire of a thousand years ago.

Behind Ghana's sandy coast there is a large tropical rain forest. Cocoa trees are grown here by about 300,000 small farmers. Ghana is the largest producer of cocoa in the world.

A large new dam on the Volta River will provide electric power for new industry. This is important, for Ghana has little coal or oil.

A large aluminum plant near the dam will process aluminum from Ghana's rich ores.

Near Accra (ah-krah'), the capital, a new seaport called Tema (Tee'mah) is being built.

There are about seven million people in Ghana. Most of them are farmers and fishermen. Many cannot read or write. The government is sending teachers out to teach the adults the things most people learn as children in schools.

Students, businessmen, and farmers still wear the colorful native dress. This is a brightly printed cotton robe, twisted around the body. The end is tossed over the left shoulder. However, men in factories and mines find that western clothes are less likely to get caught in the machinery.

The president of Ghana believes that African states should join together. He signed a union agreement with Guinea (gihn'ee) and later with Mali (mahl'ee).

opposite: Woman dressed for a wedding in Ghana

This seems like a good idea, but there are problems.

Ghana uses English as the official language. Guinea and Mali use French.

Ghana is not near either of the other two countries.

Guinea and Mali have a common border, but no roads or railroads link the two countries. Mali has a railroad to the coast, but it runs through Senegal and not through Guinea.

Guinea is larger than Ghana, but much poorer. It became completely independent of France in 1958.

above: A fleet of fishing canoes in Tema Harbor, Ghana

below: Family walking along the Niger River in Mali.
The Markala Dam in the background in one of the longest
in the world built just for soil irrigation.

Guinea's future seems to be as an industrial and mining country. A dam on the Konkoure River will provide power for aluminum and iron mills.

Mali became independent of France in 1960, but remained a member of the French Community of Nations.

Bamako (bam'ah-ko), the capital, is on the banks of the Niger River. It is a city of tree-lined avenues and large gardens. It has a famous zoo and museum.

Timbuktu (tim-buck-too'), in the north, is an ancient city. It was an oasis, or fertile area, for camel caravans traveling across the Sahara. It is still an important market city.

The life of most of the people of Mali centers around the Niger River. The land is flat. The yearly flooding of the plains has always fertilized and irrigated the land.

Now a dam has raised the river level and made much more land available for farming. Rice, cotton, and peanuts are raised and exported to other parts of tropical Africa.

Portuguese Guinea is a small tropical territory of Portugal. However few of the people are Portuguese. Rice is grown near the coast on land where mangrove swamps have been cleared. Peanuts and palm oil are exported.

below: Man surveying at the Volta Dam site. When complete, this dam will provide electrical power for new industries in many towns and villages in southern Ghana.

G. Gerster of Black Star for World Bank

Ten Newly
Independent Nations

These ten newly independent nations have two things in common. They all gained independence in 1960 and all remained part of the French Community of Nations.

Senegal, north of Portuguese Guinea, is low-lying land. Most of it is less than 650 feet above sea level. France buys its entire peanut crop. Other things are grown only for home use.

Dakar is the capital of Senegal and most of the industry is here. There is also the University of Dakar.

Upper Volta is completely landlocked. It is a poor, semi-arid country. Cattle, the major export, are driven live to Ghana.

Niger (nye'jur) is also a landlocked country. The northern section is part of the Sahara Desert. The only good farmland is the 185-mile stretch along the Niger River. Negro Africans farm along the river. Nomads in the north raise cattle.

Niger is a poor land where very few of the children go to school.

She is, however, planning to join forces with some of her neighbors to build roads. Large iron deposits can be mined if roads are built so it can be sent to markets.

The Ivory Coast is one of the richest nations in West Africa because of its coffee crop.

There are lagoons along the Atlantic coast with tropical forests beyond them. Toward the north, the land rises in rolling grassy plains.

Togo is today the smallest independent country in all Africa. At its widest point it is only 124 miles across. It

opposite: Waterfront market in Dakar, Senegal

Pan American World Airways

is a tropical country except where the land rises in the Atakora Mountains.

Most of the people in Togo are farmers. Coffee and cocoa are the chief exports.

Dahomey (dah-hoe'mee), like neighboring Togo, has a low, sandy coastline with no natural harbors. The capital, Porto Novo, is on a lagoon near the coast.

Palm trees grow beyond the coast and the Atakora Mountains cut diagonally across the country.

In upper Dahomey the Bariba tribe are great horsemen. They raise kapok and shea trees for oil from the seeds. But they measure importance by the number of horses a man owns. Less than five per cent of the people can read and write.

Cameroun (kam-ah-roon') has a tropical coast with its forest. The central region is a high plateau. There are mountains in the west, and the north is a large, flat plain.

This is a country of small farms. Farmers in the plateau region build cone-shaped huts of straw and mud.

below: Togoland children come home from school

UNESCO—Eric Schwab

The southwest highland region is the most fertile. Cocoa, palm products, bananas, coffee, and cotton are all raised here.

Chad is another landlocked country. Most of the northern section is in the Sahara and of course is very dry. The Arabs in the north and the Negro Africans in the south all raise livestock, and cotton is grown for export.

Lake Chad in the southwest is on the border of Chad, Niger, Nigeria, and Cameroun. It is only three or four feet deep. The Africans still use shallow boats made of papyrus, much as their ancestors did. Few of the people of Chad can read and write.

The Central African Republic is another poor, landlocked country. It is largely tropical rain forest. Small African pygmies live here, and also other tribes.

Some of the women of the tribes that live along the Ubangi River wear huge disks in their lips. This may have been begun to discourage Arab slave traders from taking the women, but now it is considered a mark of beauty.

Bangui (bahn-ghee), the capital, is a city of 80,000 people. Diamonds and fine tropical woods are exported.

Gabon (gah-bone') is almost all tropical rain forest. Forest pygmies were probably the original people of the country. However, now they are only a small part of the native population.

Most unusual for an African country is the fact that eighty per cent of the children of Gabon go to school.

Mahogany and ebony come from the forests. Uranium and oil are exported. Cocoa, coffee, rice, and palm products are important.

Dr. Albert Schweitzer was the most famous person in Gabon for many years. He went to Lambaréné (lahm-bah-ray'nee), a tiny village in the jungle, and set up a clinic and hospital. Whole families come with the patient. They live with him in huts around the hospital.

Dr. Schweitzer died in 1965, but the work of the hospital continues. It offers the only medical service for thousands of Africans.

John Moss of Black Star for World Bank

above right: Painter works on a bridge in the Republic of Gabon as a diesel passes

The Desert
Makes a Difference

The Sahara Desert sprawls across northern Africa from the Atlantic to the Red Sea. It is not all rolling sand dunes. A rocky ridge cuts diagonally across it. It once took a camel caravan two months to cross it. Now there are truck roads. An oasis probably has a gas station. Planes hop across the Sahara in a couple of hours.

For thousands of years, the countries around the northwest corner of Africa were cut off from the rest of the continent by the low Atlas Mountains and the desert.

Come by ocean liner in to Port Etienne in Mauritania (mawr-ah-tay'nee-ah). This is the only harbor in this harsh, 500-mile coastline. Here are Arabs and Berbers, Moors and Negro tribesmen, all in colorful native dress and speaking their own languages. Businessmen in western suits speak French. The Arab women wear veils across their faces. The Berber and Moorish women do not.

Mauritania is a land of mountain ranges and desert. There is not enough water for farming. Most Mauritanians are nomads who move from place to place to find pasture for sheep, goats, and camels. The nomads live mostly on milk, dates, and the cereal grain, millet. Camels are raised for export and for their hair. Cloth made from camel's hair is soft, light, and warm. The Moors weave the material for their black tents out of the coarser camel's hair.

Mauritania has been independent since 1960, and a member of the French Community of Nations. A new capital city is rising on the desert at Nouakchott (nou-ahk'shot). At one time there were only mud huts here.

opposite: Newly trained workman operates a winch at a mine site in Mauritania

Mauritania is a poor country but rich in minerals. The name of the mountains here—Kaedi d' Idjill—means "mountains of iron," which they are. The country's only railroad runs from Port Etienne to Fort Gourad near the mountains.

There are no surfaced roads, but there are many airfields. Even the nomads sometimes use planes to come to the city for supplies.

Spanish Sahara, north of Mauritania, is a desolate land. It has only 13,000 people and one main city. Mauritania and Morocco (mah-rahk'oh) both claim this land, but Spain has shown no desire to give it up.

Morocco, on the northwest corner of Africa, pokes a thumb of land toward Spain. This is the south gatepost of the Straits of Gibraltar.

Morocco is an ancient country. The present king, Hassan II, is a direct descendant of a king who ruled in 1649. Parts of the country were once governed by France and Spain, but it has been independent since 1956. The king is one of the few absolute rulers left in the world. Though he now has a legislative assembly, he has the power to veto anything.

Most of the people are Berbers and Arabs. The old, old cities are in the fertile plain. Rabat (rah-baht') is the capital, but Casablanca is the most important city. If you walk down the Avenue of the Royal Armed Forces, you are in a beautiful modern city. But if you go down the narrow crowded side streets, you know you are in North Africa. Veiled Moslem women hurry by. Open-air markets called bazaars offer everything for sale. There are fruits and vegetables, beautiful mosaic tiles, brass and copper pots and trays, and exquisitely embroidered fabrics.

For thousands of years, Moroccan children worked as apprentices to learn the ancient crafts. Now boys are taught these crafts at schools like the School of Popular Arts at Tetuan. Girls learn to embroider at school. Moslems are not allowed to show living things in their art. Intricate geometric designs are used.

Education is not new in Morocco. Kairaween University at Fez was founded in 859 A.D. What is new is that now so many Moroccans go to school.

The Atlas Mountains run north and south through the country. In the mountains and on the coastal plain the weather is pleasant. In the desert, however, it is hot and dry all year. An ancient caravan route across the desert linked Morocco with Timbuktu.

Algeria (al-jeer'ee-ah), like other ancient countries on the Mediterranean, is close to Europe. The city of Carthage, settled by Phoenician (fih-neesh'un) sailors, fought three wars with Rome. They fought with galley ships called triremes (try'reemz), that had three banks of oars. Rome finally won. Carthage was destroyed to the ground and never rebuilt.

opposite top: Tribesmen of the Tamawar region perform the Moroccan "Haha" dance

opposite bottom: Farmer prepares for fall planting on the Plains of Rharb in Morocco

43

Later Arabs swept across Algeria. France invaded it in 1830 and in 1848 Algeria became a part of France.

Eighty per cent of Algeria is mountain and desert.

The fertile coastal plain, 150 to 200 miles deep, was settled by Frenchmen. Arabs resented this. In 1954 the bloodiest of the African revolutions began. Eight years later Algeria became independent of France. More than half of the European population has fled.

Algiers, the capital, is called the "Paris of Africa." Most of the prosperous Frenchmen, however, have left the city. Algiers has an excellent harbor from which olive oil, citrus fruit, and wine are shipped to other parts of the world. It is a city of beautiful homes and modern buildings. But walk into the Casbah, the Arab section, and life seems not to have changed in a thousand years.

Oran is also an important seaport, a thousand years old. It is an industrial city with metal-working plants and canning factories.

Tunisia (too-nee'zhuh) is a small country of northern Africa. Like the others, its fertile plain is cut off from the desert by mountains. Most of the people are Arabs or Berbers.

There are small farms near the sea. Nomads raise flocks of sheep and mules in the drier areas.

One interesting change that has come with independence from France (1957) is that every Tunisian must have a last name. Before that time, most people had a long string of names that told who their ancestors were. A boy might be Ali ben Mohamed ben Ahmed. This meant Ali, son of Mohamed, who was the son of Ahmed.

Tunisia is a republic with a president who must be a Moslem.

Libya is a country of three provinces separated by deserts. The provinces are Tripolitania (trip-ahl-ih-tane' yah), Cyrenaica (sir-ah-nay'ah-kah), and Fezzan (feh-zan'). They are each quite different.

Tripoli is the capital of the country and the capital of Tripolitania. Fertile rolling hills are covered with vineyards and orchards. The climate is moderate.

opposite: Prize-winning sire on a farm in Libya

Arab Information Center

45

The desert separates Tripolitania and Cyrenaica, both of which are on the Mediterranean. Cyrenaica is hotter and drier country than Tripolitania. Dates are the main crop. Sheep, goats, and camels are grazed in the lowlands.

Fezzan is the inland province. It is almost completely desert except for a few oases. These oases are surprisingly fertile. There are many date palms there, and enough grass for grazing cattle.

No roads run across Fezzan to the other two provinces.

Libya has few natural resources. Oil and natural gas, however, have been discovered. It is hoped that income from oil and gas will help to pay for deep wells. Water from these wells would make more farmland possible. There is interest in building a plant for taking salt from sea water. Fresh water is the greatest need of much of Africa.

below: Kindergarten class in Tripoli, Libya

Countries of the Nile

The Nile River has written a story of its own on the continent of Africa. For thousands of years it was a mystery story.

How could a great river flow through a thousand miles of desert without rain or streams to feed it?

How could it bring from the desert enough fertile soil to build 8,000 square miles of rich land at its mouth? (The Greeks called this area the *delta* after the fourth letter of their alphabet, which is in the shape of a triangle.)

Strangest of all, how could this river flood its valley in late summer when other streams were drying up?

"The wind from the sea pushes the water back," said some. "The ocean rises and shoves the river out of its banks," said another. "Melting snow in the mountains causes it," said another. "How could that be?" they questioned him. "The farther you go upriver to the south, the hotter it gets!"

Now we know what the truth is. The mystery is solved. This 4,000 mile river begins in Lake Victoria. Heavy rains from the heart of the "dark continent" feed it. Many rivers join it. The journey to its valley is a long one, so the flood season is late. Fertile soil from the rain forests is carried to its delta.

Egypt is nearly all desert, except for the Nile Valley, the delta, and a few mountains along the Red Sea.

More than 4,000 years ago the Nile Valley was the home of one of the earliest civilizations on the earth. The story of the people of this country is a long and interesting one. Probably more has happened to their way of living in the last twenty years than in the several thousand years before.

Egypt has been a republic since 1953. It is governed by a president and a national assembly.

It has been the dream of President Nasser to unite the Arab world. He has not succeeded in this, but he has changed the official name of Egypt to the United Arab

Republic. The old name that is more familiar to us is used in this book.

Since 1869 ships have not had to go around the continent of Africa to get to India. The Suez Canal in eastern Egypt now connects the Mediterranean with the Gulf of Suez and the Red Sea. For many years it was operated by a private company under the watchful eye of England. In 1956 Egypt took over the canal. It continues to be the busiest canal in the world.

The busy seaport of Alexandria, on the delta, was founded by Alexander the Great more than three hundred years before the birth of Christ.

opposite: Convoy leaves Lake Timsah, about halfway through the 100-mile Suez Canal

below: Construction workers widen and deepen the Suez Canal

A camel drinks at a waterhole
in the United Arab Republic
(Egypt)

This beautiful city drowses in the sun. There are miles of beautiful beaches. Modern apartment buildings look down on ruins of buildings that were new when the early Greeks and Romans occupied the city.

If you go up the Nile from Alexandria you come to Cairo, the bustling, modern capital. Here are new hotels, television stations, government buildings and luxurious apartments. Cairo has much in common with any modern city. But outside the city in the desert are those man-made mountains, the pyramids. About eighty of them still stand on the west bank of the Nile. They were built by kings, called pharaohs (feh'roze), of ancient Egypt.

Moslems kneel to pray before a
mosque in Alexandria, Egypt

An Egyptian artist works on his
delicate design at the Khan
Khalili Bazaar

These were tombs that would be safe from robbers, animals, and floods. But what ancient Egyptians were able to build, robbers were able to break into. The gold and jewels buried with a pharaoh are gone.

The largest pyramid stood almost forty stories high and covered thirteen acres. The Sphinx still guards the empty tombs.

You can follow the Nile inland for hundreds of miles before you are stopped by the first falls at Aswan.

Peasants in the floodplains along the river still plant, weed, and harvest their crops by hand. But there is change stirring here as new methods are introduced. Fine Egyp-

The Nile River at Aswan flows
toward the sea

tian cotton cloth is now being made in factories rather than on hand looms.

At Aswan an enormous dam is being built. It will control the flooding of the Nile, and make a million and a half more acres of land available for farming.

The dam, to be finished by 1970, will also back up the river into a lake 175 miles long. Unfortunately this land has two ancient temples on it. They were carved out of the mountainside by Rameses II, 3,200 years ago. Four colossal statues of Rameses, sixty-five feet high, stare out across the desert from the front of the temples. When the lake reaches its depth of 250 feet, these temples would be under water.

Teams of workmen from sixteen nations have begun to cut these statues and temples into pieces and to free them from the mountain. By 1969 both temples should be completely restored on the top of the cliff, far above the rising water.

The new dam will not only give Egypt controlled water for farming, but it will provide electric power for the whole country and its growing industries.

About a hundred miles upriver from the temples of Rameses II are the second falls of the Nile. This marks the boundary of Sudan.

The Blue Nile and the White Nile come together at Khartoum (Car-toom'), the capital, and form the Nile.

The people in northern Sudan are Arabs, and most of them are nomads. Except along the Nile, the country is desert.

Southern Sudan has a vast swamp land at its center, and the people are Negroid Africans.

Sudan became a free nation in 1956. It has two ports on the Red Sea.

opposite top: A woman cotton picker works in the irrigated land in the Gezira plains of Sudan, where cotton is the most important income-producing crop

opposite bottom: Ruins of the Temple of Luxor, built in Egypt by Rameses II 3200 years ago

Ethiopia and Somalia

Ethiopia (ee-thee-oh'pee-ah) is east of Sudan. For many years it was a little-known, landlocked country, ringed by mountains. Now airplanes and two ports on the Red Sea link this country with the outside world.

The Rift Valley runs across Ethiopia, the center of which is a high plateau, ending in steep slopes on the northwest.

Lake Tana is the source of the Blue Nile which winds across the high plateau before it drops to join the White Nile in Sudan. It has cut gorges in the plateau 4,000 feet deep in some places.

There are two railroads in Ethiopia. And many surfaced roads radiate from Addis Ababa, the capital. Airplanes, however, are the most important means of transportation.

The emperor claims to be descended from Menelik I, who was supposed to be the son of King Solomon and the Queen of Sheba. The people are Hamitic (hah-mit'ik) and Semitic (seh-mit'ik). Most of them are herdsmen raising zebu cattle, sheep, and horses. The cash crop is coffee.

Wrapped around Ethiopia on the east is Somalia (so-mahl'ee-ah). It is shaped like the number 7. The top is on the Gulf of Aden. It was formerly British Somaliland. The long part of the 7 slants down along the Indian Ocean. This part was Italian Somaliland. The two countries united in 1960 as independent Somalia.

Animals are regarded as wealth. The nomads who raise cattle, sheep, and camels never want to part with any, even the sickliest.

In the tropical south, between the Juba and the Shebeli rivers, bananas and sugar cane are raised.

Like many African countries, Somalia has fourteen airfields but no railroads. The few roads are completely

opposite: Falls of the Blue Nile in Ethiopia

54

impassable in the two rainy seasons. They get monsoons here—storms with wind and rain that raise havoc with fishing fleets along the sea.

Between Somalia and Ethiopia, on the Gulf of Aden, there is the little country of French Somaliland. It is a crossroads of shipping for the world. The railroad from Ethiopia crosses French Somaliland to the harbor. Much of this country suffers from lack of water, and so most of the people are nomads. In the fertile areas, vegetables and dates are grown.

opposite: Worker in an Ethiopian fiber mill at Addis Ababa

Elephants Have the Right of Way— the Tropical East Coast

Our route has taken us clear around the continent from the Republic of South Africa. Now we are back on the tropical east coast where the ancient Arabs came looking for slaves and ivory.

The coastal plain along the Indian Ocean is from ten to forty miles wide.

In Kenya the coastal plain is a land of coconut trees and rain forests.

The rising coastal plain becomes a high plateau about 300 miles inland. This is 10,000 feet high in some places.

The plateau is slashed by the Rift Valley. It is a broad, flat valley in the north. Farther south the valley is deep and narrow between high cliffs.

To the west, the plateau descends to the plains around Lake Victoria.

Most of the people of Kenya live in the high country. The bustling, modern cities are here. Nairobi is the capital.

Mombasa (mahm-bahs′ah), on the Indian Ocean, is the port of entry for Kenya. Here you can join a safari and head for big game country. Go to one of the many national parks in Kenya—at Nairobi, Tsavo, Mt. Kenya, or Amboseli. This last one, at the foot of Mount Kilimanjaro, is home to five thousand elephants, protected from hunters.

There are also zebras, lions, giraffes, rhinos, hippos, crocodiles, and many other animals on the Kenya plains and along the rivers.

Kenya became self-governing in 1963. It had been one of the four territories of British East Africa.

Much of the best farmland is in what is called the "white highlands." For a long time, all this good land was owned

opposite: Rhinos relax on the sandy plains of Kenya

by Europeans. The largest native tribe, the Kikuyu, were confined to reservations between the two sections of good land. Resentment exploded in the Mau-Mau terrors of 1950, and many people were killed.

Most of the export crops come from these highlands, and African farmers can now own land there.

The Masai (mah-sye') are the most unusual of the native cattle raisers. They count their wealth in cattle and do not kill them for meat. They live on grain and milk mixed with blood. Once every two or three weeks they shoot an arrow with a curved head into the jugular vein of a cow. They catch the blood in a gourd and slap mud over the wound. The cow then rejoins the herd.

Burlap-clad chimpanzee at Kenya

Boys watch road construction
in Kenya

Men of Kenya weighing tea
leaves in Ragati

Like many dry countries, much of Kenya's arid land has been ruined by over-grazing. Now the Africans are working together to save it. They terrace it, plant it with hardy grass, and do not over-graze it.

Uganda, west of Kenya, lies between Lake Victoria and the Sudan. It rises in the west in the "Mountains of the Moon."

On the equator, it is high enough to be warm but not hot.

It is possible to travel any way you like in Uganda. Air service is everywhere in Africa. Steamers ply Lake Victoria and other lakes, and part of the Victoria Nile. The Uganda system of roads is one of the best.

below: A concrete disc marks the spot where the equator crosses Uganda

opposite: View of Mt. Kilimanjaro in Tanganyika

If you drive through Queen Elizabeth National Park you will see road signs warning that "Elephants Have the Right of Way."

Most of the hippopotamuses of the world live in this country. The rare white rhinoceros is found here too.

The Buganda are the largest tribe in this country, with more than a million people. The king, or kabaka, of the Buganda province was elected president of Uganda in 1963, a year after the country won independence from Britain.

Kampala is the capital and the University College of East Africa is there.

Major exports are coffee, cotton, and copper.

Tanzania (tan-zan'yah) is a new nation, a union of Tanganyika and the island of Zanzibar.

Tanganyika has always been a tropical African country. Zanzibar has been ruled by the Arabs who live there, and has more kinship with the East.

Lake Victoria, on the northern boundary of Tanganyika, and Lake Tanganyika, one of the deepest lakes in the world, both lie in the Rift Valley.

The teeth and skull of a stone-age man have been found in the Olduvai Gorge (ohl'dah-way).

The capital, Dar es Salaam, is a busy port on the Indian Ocean. Gold, diamonds, and agricultural products are shipped from here. The city boasts of a new university.

All through Tanzania people are learning to vote and to drive tractors. Sisal (sye'sahl), used in making rope, is one of the major products of the country. Cotton, coffee, and tobacco are also raised for export.

Hundreds of the wild African animals are found in certain areas. Antelope, zebra, elephant, hippopotamus, giraffe, lion, leopard, and cheetah. Monkeys are plentiful. The wild animal preserve in Serengati National Park is very well known.

Before 1962, the independent countries of Rwanda (roo-ahn' dah) and Burundi (buh-roon' dee) were a Belgian Trust Territory called Ruanda-Urundi.

These two small, high-plateau countries are six hundred miles from the sea. Western boundaries are along Lake Tanganyika and the Congo.

A few pygmy groups live in the jungles. But up to eighty-four per cent of the people in both lands are Bahutu —farmers and cattle raisers. They live in grass huts the shape of beehives.

The small percentage of Watusi (wah-too' see) living here are among the most interesting of African people. Most of them are slender, six or seven feet tall. It is thought that they came originally from the Nile Valley and migrated to the Sudan and then to Ethiopia.

About four hundred years ago they moved into the Rwanda-Burundi area. Although they were outnumbered eight to one, they were fierce warriors and conquered the land. A Watusi king, or Mwani, ruled each country.

In Rwanda, after independence, thousands of Watusi were killed and many others fled to neighboring countries.

The Bahutu and the Watusi get along better in Burundi. The Watusi Mwani is still head of the government there.

The tribal dancing of the Watusi is one of the most colorful sights in Africa.

opposite: Fishing boats line the shore of Lake Victoria, Africa's largest lake. In the background a lake steamer is docked.

Africa is a huge, beautiful, restless continent. It is a land of deserts, jungles, high plateaus, and endless grasslands.

It is home to elephant, giraffe, and zebra.

It is a continent of people, and of many new, independent nations. Something is stirring from the heart of the modern cities to the remote jungle villages. A continent awakening often finds the process painful.

Africa is a land of contrasts. It is rich and it is poor. It is backward and it is booming. The past is often present. But the future looms bright.

above: An African hunter

right: Thatched-roof huts in a native village in Freetown, Sierre Leone

top: Palm trees border the coast road of Lagos, Nigeria

bottom: Natives in colorful outfits shop in the market place in Accra, Ghana

right: Panorama of the modern city of Johannesburg, South Africa

Decorated mud walls
enclosing each house of
the Ndebele Tribe.
Vegetable dye or local
colored stone is used
for color, South Africa

right: The lion and lioness are feared by other animals, Kenya

below: Herd of zebras in Kenya. No two zebras have identical stripes

Nita Engle—Hollis Associates

opposite:
A native
gets water from
a small pond
in Somali

right: The tusks
of an elephant
are valuable
trophies
for the hunter

Photo by Scott Callier

Pan American Airways

Photo by Mehmet Ileri

Photo by Joan Sullivan

opposite:
Fertile land
in Marrakech,
Morocco

above left: Mosaic
patterns in
the Green Mosque,
Bursa, Turkey

left: A veiled
Moslem woman
in Jordan

Srinagar lies along
the banks of the
Jhelum River which is
crossed by seven
bridges, Kashmir

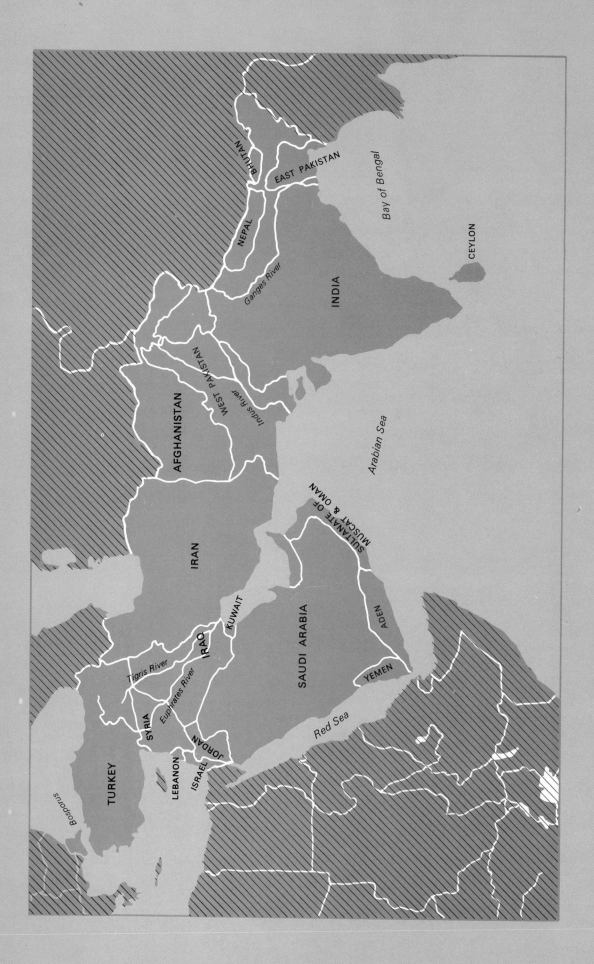

The Arabian Peninsula

The continent of Asia sprawls over a third of the globe. It is home to two-thirds of all the people in the world. You cannot see all this land, nor meet all the people in one trip. But you can make a start by going east from Africa into southwest Asia.

This non-oriental part of Asia is sometimes called the Middle East.

In no more time than it takes to cross the Red Sea from Africa, you are in Saudi (saw'dee) Arabia. Jiddah (jihd'ah), with its quarter of a million people, is the main port on the Red Sea.

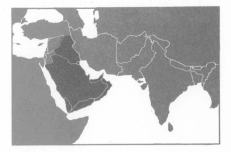

On a map, Saudi Arabia is on a peninsula that looks like a Stone-Age ax, attached by its thick neck to the rest of Asia. Ancient caravans crossed this broad neck of land over some of the oldest trade routes in the world.

Saudi Arabia is a land of deserts, so of course is very dry. The largest one is called Rub'al-Khali—the Empty Quarter—and covers a third of the country. Even the coastal plain is dry. There are no rivers or lakes in this country. There are only a few oases with their springs. The desert is no fit place to live, but sometimes you can see nomads riding their swift horses or racing their camels across the hot, shifting sand dunes.

Until recently, the camel was the usual way of getting across the deserts. Roads are now being built, and cars and trucks are sometimes seen outside the big cities. A short railroad runs from the capital, Riyadh (ree-yahd'), to Dammam (dah-mam') on the Persian Gulf. The Hijaz Railroad was owned by Turkey during World War I. T. E. Lawrence, the Englishman called Lawrence of Arabia, led Arab troops in sweeping raids across the desert and destroyed the railroad and drove out the Turks. This railroad has been in operation again only since 1963.

opposite: Map of Asia. Areas in darker color will be discussed in this book.

Saudi Arabia is the seat of the Moslem religion. Medina and Mecca are the holy cities. For many years the main income of the country came from taxes paid by Moslems making a pilgrimage to Mecca. Few Europeans have ever visited Mecca. For many years it was death to any non-Moslem who was caught within its walls.

Now Saudi Arabia has large oil fields. Most of the income of the country comes from oil.

The country itself is named for the Sa'ud family. Chief Ibn Sa'ud conquered a number of tribes and cities and made himself, and his family, rulers of most of the Arabian peninsula. It was not until 1932 that the country as we know it today, was finally brought together. Ibn Sa'ud died in 1953, but his son still rules as absolute monarch. All slaves were freed in 1962.

below: A Saudi Arabian father reads to his sons from the Koran, the Moslem Bible

Arab Information Center

There are several little countries around the south end of the Arabian peninsula.

Yemen, on the Red Sea, is a little pie-shaped, mountainous country. It is a poor country which seems to have no oil. The people live much as their ancestors did for centuries.

The coastal region of Yemen is hot and dry. Most of the people live in straw huts. In the cooler mountains, the huts are usually made of mud or stone. The better houses have a lower story of sandstone, granite, or basalt with upper stories made of mud. The roof often has an open gallery topped with brass. Here the women of the family can sit and watch the world go by without being seen. Yemen is a Moslem country. It became a republic in 1962. Coffee is the major export.

below: The Dammam-Dhahran Highway in Saudi Arabia is surfaced with a combination of local rock and asphalt

Arab Information Center

Just south of Yemen are the crown colony of Aden (ahd'n) and the Protectorate of South Arabia. These make up what we think of as Aden. The town of Aden, two small townships, and a few islands make up the crown colony. Aden has a good harbor and is a fueling port-of-call for ships going through the Suez Canal.

The Protectorate of South Arabia extends along the arid coastal strip. High plateaus and mountain ranges rise in back of this. Very little of the land can be farmed. Most people are nomads, following their goats, sheep, and camels. Travel is by donkey or camel caravan, or by the small Arab boat called a *dhow* along the seacoast.

The Sultanate of Muscat and Oman curves around the eastern side of the Arabian peninsula. It is a small country with a thousand miles of coastline. It is mostly barren mountains and bleak desert. Some oil has been discovered on this poor land. This may bring it prosperity.

Little Kuwait (kah-wate'), just north of Saudi Arabia on the Persian Gulf, has the richest oil fields in the world.

Before oil was discovered, most of the people lived in small mud huts. The Emir, or ruler, and his court lived in larger houses of coral and limestone. Now little Kuwait receives hundreds of millions of dollars from the oil companies. The people have free schools, medical care, and many other things. The government is building better homes for them, and poor families are being helped to buy their own homes.

Water has always been scarce. Now in Kuwait six million gallons of fresh water per day come from a plant that removes the salt from sea water in order to make it all right for drinking.

Kuwaiti shipbuilders have been making deep-water dhows for hundreds of years. Pearl fishermen still dive in the waters of the Persian Gulf, but this is not so important as it once was.

Kuwait is considered an Arab state. A constitution was adopted in 1963 that provided for a National Assembly. The emir is now a constitutional monarch. The assembly can override his veto of a bill.

Iraq is just north of Kuwait. The Greeks called the northern part of this land Mesopotamia, which means the "Land Between Two Rivers." The rivers are the Tigris and the Euphrates (you-fray'teez). They flow diagonally down through this country like the two tines of a tuning fork, then join forces and flow into the Persian Gulf.

The rivers, over the years, brought fertile soil from the mountains. The green valley became the site of one of the earliest civilizations on earth. Babylon and Nineveh were bustling cities in Bible times. Baghdad became the crossroads of caravan routes.

More than caravans came from Baghdad. Wonderful stories came from there, too. It is said that long, long ago a sultan was going to put his wife to death in the morning. But she told him a story—spun him a tale—that delighted him so much he wanted her to tell him another the next night. And the next, and the next, for a thousand and one nights. The queen was saved because the sultan could not live without her stories of Sinbad, and Ali Baba and the Forty Thieves, and all the other stories of the "Arabian Nights!"

below: Sinbad's Watch Tower in Iraq

opposite: Basrah market scene shows the color and variety of people and goods found in Iraq

left: Oil wells in Iraq are illuminated by the flames from burning gases

Baghdad is still a crossroad of the world. But now there is the Baghdad-Berlin Railroad, an international airport, and modern buildings and taxicabs. But also there are still colorful bazaars and open-air cafes lining the Tigris.

Oil is the most important mineral in Iraq. Foreign oil companies give half their earnings to the government.

The farmers and nomad cattle-grazers in the north-eastern mountains of Iraq are Kurds. They have more in common with the Kurds in Turkey than with the rest of the country of Iraq. Recently, they have been fighting the government because they want to rule themselves.

South of the Euphrates River are Arab nomads who belong to the Bedouin tribes. They are desert people with a stern way of life.

The shepherds of the Euphrates valley do not belong to the desert tribes. But they are nomads and drive their flocks from pasture to pasture.

Marsh Arabs live in the permanently flooded marshes in the south of Iraq. They live mainly on fish, rice, water-birds, and water buffaloes.

Two-thirds of this land of rivers is now desert and high treeless plains. Now the money from oil will help restore old irrigation systems, build new ones, and double the usable farmland.

87

Bible Land

Follow one of the old caravan routes from Baghdad east to the Mediterranean. Ports along this stretch of sea were gateways between the riches of the east and the markets of the west. Armies have fought over this land, coming from first one way and then another. Great ideas were born in this land and have spread to the ends of the earth. This much fought-over part of the world is now sacred to Jews, Christians, and Moslems.

The tiny country of Palestine was split in 1948 and became Israel, a new Jewish state, and Jordan, an Arab kingdom. The Arab states did not recognize the legality of Israel. Fighting broke out. The two countries still live side by side in a very uneasy peace.

Most of Israel's cities are along the fertile coastal plain. Here, too, are the fields and groves and vineyards. Inland from the coast, the hills rise dry and desolate. Much of this old, worn-out land is being reclaimed by irrigation.

The Jordan Valley is a northern extension of the great Rift Valley that cuts through Africa. It is probably the most dramatic feature of this Bible Land.

The Jordan River begins in the mountains of Lebanon and flows to the Sea of Galilee. Then it continues in a winding course to end in the Dead Sea, which is more than a thousand feet below sea level. The Dead Sea has no outlet. The hot sun causes the water to evaporate and more and more minerals brought by the river are left in the lake. Even salt-water fish cannot live in this water. This low, salty sea in the great rift is 1200 feet deep.

South of the Dead Sea the Negev Desert extends to the Gulf of Aqaba on the Red Sea. Bedouin nomads follow their flocks across the sands. They still live in black tents as they did in Bible times.

opposite: Peaceful view of the Sea of Galilee in Israel, where little has changed since Biblical times.

Abraham with his wandering tribe, similar to the Bedouins, came from the "Land Between Two Rivers," and settled at the edge of the Negev. This was two thousand years before the birth of Christ.

Men have found some of King Solomon's copper mines in the wilderness of the Negev.

The boundary line between Israel and Jordan runs through the city of Jerusalem. Barbed wire and soldiers guard the line, and visitors may cross it only once. Since

most of the holy places are on the Jordan side of the line, it is well to start a tour of the Holy Land in Jordan.

Shepherds and camel caravans show that many people in Jordan still live as they did in Bible times.

In Jordan you may see the site of Solomon's temple and of Calvary. Here is the church of the Holy Sepulcher, built above the tomb of Jesus. The first church was built here in the fourth century. It was rebuilt by the Crusaders after they captured Jerusalem in 1099. Today the church is shared by different sects.

The Moslem Dome of the Rock is built over the spot where Solomon's Temple stood. Its altar is the rock where Abraham prepared to sacrifice Isaac, his only son. This is also a holy spot for Moslems who believe that the Prophet Mohammed, founder of their religion, rose up from the rock to heaven, leaving his footprint in the stone. This is the most important Moslem shrine, next to Mecca and Medina.

Bethlehem still dreams under the brilliant sun. Narrow streets wind up the two hills. Bethlehem was a market town long before the birth of Christ. Its name means "House of Bread," and the round, flat loaves of Biblical times are still baked in its ovens.

When the three kings came from the east to Bethlehem, they searched until they found the Christ child lying in a manger in a small cave, or grotto. The Church of the Nativity, the oldest Christian church still in use, was built above the grotto in 325 A.D. by the Roman Emperor Constantine. This church is the only one in the Holy Land not destroyed by later conquerors of the country.

Inside the church, a dark narrow staircase leads down into the Grotto of the Nativity.

People in Bethlehem still live in houses built above small caves like this one. The caves are at ground level and the animals live in them. The family lives in a room one flight up.

opposite: This oasis in Jordan provides water and shelter for desert travelers and their animals

The mountains of Moab still look down on the oasis of Jericho, whose walls came tumbling down when Joshua's trumpets blew, about 1200 B.C. Biblical Jericho is no more. But the oasis still has a village of Arabs and a camp of Arab refugees who fled from Israel.

About a million and a half people live in Jordan, where the hills of Judea and Samaria rise to about 3000 feet, and where the Jordan valley drops to more than a thousand feet below sea level. About a quarter of a million people live in Amman, the capital. About sixty thousand people live in the part of Jerusalem that is in Jordan. There are more than half a million Arab refugees from Israel in Jordan.

below: A colorful "Sous" (lemonade) vendor displays his goods. He carries two brass plates that he uses to make a clanging noise to attract customers.

High on its hills, the old Jerusalem is in Jordan. Here are the old stone walls and narrow streets and stairways.

The Jerusalem of Israel is the capital of the new country. New suburbs sprawl to the south. Here, as everywhere in the country, it is hard to separate past and present. All through the country the land is being restored. New copper mines are being worked near the site of King Solomon's mines.

Acre (ahk'er), on the northern coast, is an ancient seaport. It remains one of the best ports in Israel. Richard the Lion-Hearted, the English king who appears in the Tales of Robin Hood, captured Acre from the Moslems.

below left: Small boy sits astride his donkey at the Amman market in Jordan

below right: A smiling Arab in Jordan proudly wears the national headdress and robes

Arab Information Center

93

Arab Information Center

above: Street in the city of Tel Aviv, Israel

opposite: This narrow twisting street in Nazareth seems unchanged since the time of Jesus more than 1900 years ago. Donkeys, as you can see, are still used for transportation.

Here in this bustling city, the ruins of a Crusader fort look down on a white Moslem mosque.

The old port of Jaffa, which may have been founded by one of the sons of Noah, now joins the modern city of Tel Aviv (tell'ah-veev) where new history is being made.

Much of the old, worn-out land of Israel is being restored by irrigation and modern farming methods.

Nazareth, nestled in its valley, climbs the surrounding hills in a series of terraces. This is the only one of the Christian holy places in Israel. It is also the largest Arab town in Israel. The narrow streets with their open shops are still much the same as they were two thousand years ago. The Virgin's Spring, the well in the center of Nazareth, is the same well from which Mary drew water for her family.

94

above: Seafront apartments high on a cliff in Beirut, Lebanon

British Overseas Airways Corporation

Bible land extends north of Israel into the little country of Lebanon and into Syria. Lebanon is bordered on the east and north by Syria.

Lebanon has an area of only about 4,000 square miles and a population of about a million and a half. Many Lebanese are Arabs, but it is a Christian country, too. The old biblical cities of Tyre and Sidon are still lived in.

Lebanon was once the holy land of the Phoenicians. These ancient inhabitants were great sailors who sailed as far as England and along the coast of Africa about 1700 B.C.

Beirut (bay-root'), capital of Lebanon, is a city of about half a million people. Here is the American University and the French Jesuit University St. Joseph. Beirut is a beautiful coastal city with many new western-style apartment buildings.

About half the people of Lebanon live on farms. A few cattle are raised for dairy purposes.

The Biga Valley lies between two mountain ranges—the Lebanon range and the Anti-Lebanon range. Mountains cause the winds from the Mediterranean to drop their rain along the shore. Inland areas are drier, although they get more rain than much of Asia.

Few of the ancient cedars of Lebanon still exist. But the government has been planting cedar seedlings high in the mountains. They plan to reforest still another half-million acres. The new forests will provide wood for building, for charcoal, and—most important—to prevent floods and soil erosion.

below: The legendary cedars of Lebanon

Syrians claim that Damascus, the capital, is the oldest city in the world that has been lived in continuously since it was founded. No one knows for sure how old Damascus is, but it is mentioned in the book of Genesis. The Street Called Straight in Damascus is an old Roman road and it is still lined with the shops and stalls of the Damascus bazaar.

Damascus changed hands several times during the long course of history. It was capital of the Arab world for almost 300 years.

For three years Syria joined Egypt as the United Arab Republic. Syria broke off this tie with Egypt in 1961, and is now called officially the Syrian Arab Republic.

Latakia is the only port in Syria into which ocean shipping can come. The one small airfield handles only local traffic.

Most Syrians still make their living from agriculture. Some cattle, goats, and sheep are raised by Arab nomads. Oil has been discovered but is not yet producing much. The most important industries are the textile industries. Almost 6000 handweavers produce the famous Damascus brocade.

above left: The entrance of the great Omayyad Mosque in Damascus. In the background, framed by the huge doorway, is one of the entrances to the dark and fascinating street bazaars.

---

opposite: The Eastern Gate, built by the Romans, leads to the old city of Damascus and the Street Called Straight. In this area are made the silk brocades, inlaid furniture, and copper and brass objects sold around the world.

Turkey

There is much that is old, and much that is new in Turkey.

In the mountains where the Tigris and the Euphrates rivers begin there is a mountain called Ararat. This, the Bible says, is where Noah landed his ark as the waters of the flood went down.

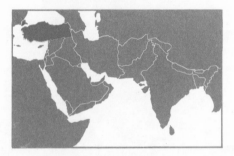

Over in the northeast corner of Turkey scientists have discovered the ancient city of Troy. In fact, they have uncovered nine cities—one on top of the other. For hundreds of years we knew of Troy only from an ancient Greek poem by Homer. He told of how the Greeks captured Troy. They built a big wooden horse and filled it with soldiers and left it at the gate. When the horse was taken into Troy itself, the soldiers jumped out and captured the city.

Another old Greek story tells how a god fell in love with a beautiful human girl named Europa. He turned himself into a white bull and, with Europa on his back, swam from Asia to a new continent. We call this continent Europe after the lovely girl. The place the bull swam across is the Bosporus, which means bull-carry in Greek.

Turkey is partly European. European Turkey is separated from Asiatic Turkey by the Straits of Dardanelles, the Sea of Marmara, and the Bosporus, which leads into the Black Sea. The Black Sea lies along the north of Turkey, the Mediterranean along the south, and the Aegean along the west.

Near the place where the bull swam the Bosporus there was an old Greek city called Byzantium. The Roman emperor Constantine rebuilt the city, renamed it Constantinople, and made it the capital. Constantinople was a rich city and many of the buildings built by the Christian Roman emperors still stand. The greatest of these is the church, Santa Sophia, built in the sixth century by Emperor

opposite: Ruins of an old Roman theater in Turkey

Justinian. The high dome is supported by 107 columns, some of them taken from earlier Greek temples.

About forty years before Columbus discovered America, Turks swept out of Asia and captured the country. Sultan Suleiman the Magnificent built the beautiful Blue Mosque.

Kemal Ataturk started the modernization of Turkey after World War I. He changed the name of Constantinople to Istanbul and moved the capital to Ankara.

Turkey has mountains in the north and south with a high central plateau. The climate varies. It is warm along the Mediterranean and cool in the plateau region.

About 97 per cent of Turkey is in Asia and most of the 30,000,000 people live here.

Farmers raise wheat and barley on the plateau, tobacco along the Aegean Sea, and figs, olives, cotton, and fruit in the south. Herdsmen take their angora goats into the dry rocky hills in the summer and bring them back to the valleys in the winter. New dams are making irrigation water available to more land and modern farming methods are being introduced. Agriculture in Turkey has more than doubled in the last fifteen years.

The valley of Goerme is one of the strangest places in the world. Here strange rock chimneys and cones of pumice have been carved out of the porous rock by action of the wind and water. Whole communities of Christian monks took refuge here when Arab, Turk, and Moslem invaders swept into the land. The monks carved out chapels and sleeping cells, connected by long tunnels. Even tables and benches were carved out of the porous stone. On the walls of the rock chapels are painted holy pictures. They still glow with color after hundreds of years.

opposite, top left: A bird's eye view of the New Mosque Eminoni and the Galata Bridge in Istanbul, Turkey

opposite, top right: Fishing nets dry in the sun near the Bosphorus in Turkey

opposite bottom: The cliff-clinging city of Antalya, Turkey

Three Moslem Countries

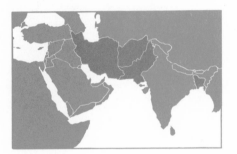

Iran is about twice as big as Turkey. Its mountainous northwest corner joins Turkey. The Caspian Sea touches the northern boundary of Iran. In the south, the country lies along the Persian Gulf, across from Saudi Arabia.

The country we now know as Iran was known as Persia throughout its long history. At one time the great Persian empire spread from the Bosporus to India.

Most of present Iran is a high, dry plateau. The plateau is from 3000 to 5000 feet high. A third of it is a salt desert. Mountains ring it along the north and west boundaries.

The civilizations in the "Land Between Two Rivers," and along the Nile were several hundred years old when horsemen swept out of the north and settled on the high plateau. They called themselves Irani (Aryan). The people still call themselves Irani, and this is how the country got its name.

Most of the rivers in Iran run to salt lakes on the interior. There is enough grass in the mountains to feed the nomads' herds of sheep and goats. About one-fourth of the people are nomads. Any oasis on the plateau becomes the site of a village. There is some farming done with irrigation. Farmers get the water from underground springs.

The coast along the Caspian Sea gets lots of rain. Here rice, tea, tobacco, and fruit are grown. There are beautiful beach resorts along this sea. Most important, however, is the commercial fishing. The famous sturgeon is caught here and smoked and sent all over the world. Sturgeon roe (eggs) are carefully salted and known as caviar—one of the most expensive foods in the world. The best caviar comes from Iran.

There are many different types of people in Iran—soldiers with fierce, bristling moustaches; women wrapped in the long black veil called the *tchador;* girls in western dress; Kurds and nomads; weavers and craftsmen; farmers and businessmen.

Mr. Pierre Streit of Black Star for World Bank

Because Iran is so hot in the summer, the houses are built to stay cool. The wealthy have summer houses in the mountains. The poorer people retreat to underground rooms during the hottest part of the day. It can be cold in winter, though, and most buildings do not have central heating. Some have small American oil heaters. But most simple homes have a *kursi*, a framework of wood with quilts thrown over it. This is set over a charcoal fire in a shallow pan, called a brazier. Snuggling down into the quilts keeps you nice and warm.

Tehran (tay-ah-rahn′) was only a sleepy village when it became the capital of the country in 1796. Now it is a bustling modern city. The shah, who is the ruler, is now a

below: Old and new, machine and mule, live side by side in Iran

constitutional monarch. He lives in Tehran in the palace of Golestan. This palace is also a museum, filled with fine rugs and ancient art objects.

Two gilded thrones, one of them the famous Peacock Throne, are among its treasures. The thrones were covered originally with emeralds and other jewels. Now many of them have been sold and replaced by imitations.

If you travel southeast from Tehran, you can visit many of the famous cities of Iran. These are sometimes called the "porcelain cities" because mosques and other buildings are decorated in porcelain tiles. The tile-maker first draws the design on paper. Then he places different-colored pieces of porcelain on the design and pours plaster over all—an ancient art brought up to date.

A hundred miles south of Tehran is Qum (koom). Most Irani make a pilgrimage to Qum. Here at the Mosque of Fateme Ma'sume (Fatima the Chaste, who died in the ninth century) you can see a cross-section of Iran. Here are Arab sheiks with white turbans, descendants of Mohammed with black turbans, and those who have made a pilgrimage to Mecca with green turbans.

From Qum, fly to Isfahan, a royal city built around an oasis, 3000 feet up in the mountains. The Ali-Kapi, royal palace of the shah, has walls covered with delicate drawings. The Palace of the Eight Paradises is made of small rooms and alcoves, each more beautifully decorated than the last. The Seminary of the Mother of the Shah, built in the early eighteenth century, has been completely restored. Its bright green and blue cupola shines in the sun.

Two famous bridges cross the Zayendeh-Rud River that runs through Isfahan. Isfahan was originally two cities. One was named Yahudiye, meaning Jewish. Iranians will tell you it got its name from the Jewish prisoners brought back from Jerusalem by Nebuchadnezzar (nehb-ah-kahd-nehz'ahr).

Shiraz, the city of roses and poets, is 300 miles from Isfahan, in a valley above the Allah-Akbar pass. It is a

opposite left: Aerial view of a dam in the rugged mountains of southwest Iran

opposite right: Aerial view of a new road in Iran

Khuzestan Water & Power Authority for World Bank   KAMPSAK

mingling of the oriental past and the present. Delicious grapes grow on the surrounding countryside. Many famous Persian poets are buried here. Near the grave of Saadi is a spring that contains sacred fish. On the last Wednesday of the Moslem Year, the sins of all who bathe in the sacred waters are washed away.

Mashhad is the greatest place of pilgrimage in Iran. Nearly every day about a thousand pilgrims visit the tomb of Ali-Reza, who was poisoned in the ninth century. The name of the city means "tomb of the martyr."

The small town of Nishapur, forty-two miles southwest of Mashhad, was the home of Omar Khayyam. He was an astronomer and poet. Although he devised a calendar more accurate than the one we use now, he is best known for his poems, called *The Rubáiyát*.

The land along the Gulf of Oman and the Persian Gulf is hot and humid, although it has little rain.

Oil is important to modern Iran. From the field at the head of the Persian Gulf it is piped to Abadan to the biggest oil refinery in the world. Although outside companies operate the oil business, half of all Iran's oil income goes to the government. In 1957 an oil field was opened at Qum.

In this country with more than 2000 years of history, there are still camel trails, but good modern roads are being built. A railroad joins the Persian Gulf and the Caspian Sea. It burrows its way through the mountains and crosses countless bridges on its travels through this rugged land.

The wonderful Persian crafts are being revived. Beautiful Persian rugs are still handwoven by weavers whose families have been weaving for centuries. The rugs are made of wool or silk of traditional patterns that have been handed down through the different tribes. In the villages, each craft has its own section of the bazaar.

There is much beauty in Iran. Light dances on the tiled buildings and roses bloom in the tiny walled gardens that are part of nearly every home.

Afghanistan, east of Iran, is a little smaller than Turkey. It is a high, landlocked country of mountains and central highlands. Russia crouches on its north. Pakistan embraces it on the east and south. Perhaps embrace is not the word to use. There have been many political arguments along the border. Every spring Nomad tribes from Pakistan move into the Afghan highlands. Every fall Afghan nomads cross over the Khyber (kye′behr) Pass into the warmer Indus Valley in Pakistan.

The low southwest corner of Afghanistan is desert. And much of the country is too rugged, rocky, and dry for use. There is a little farming in the valleys, and millions of dollars are being spent on irrigation to extend the productive land. Many of the people are nomads, and the green mountain meadows are dotted with their sheep.

There are no railroads in Afghanistan and few roads. People travel over the mountain trails by yak or camel.

Afghanistan was a Buddhist country until the middle of the eighth century, when Moslems came. A buried Buddhist temple, uncovered in the Ghorband Valley has many niches. The niches had murals painted in them and clay figures fastened to their walls. The figures were once brightly colored, with gold leaf covering the faces.

Across the Hindu Kush, the highest mountain range in Afghanistan, is the Bamian Valley. Two huge Buddhas were cut out of the rock in the vertical wall of the valley. The larger Buddha towers some 170 feet high. One of the hands, now missing, was originally raised in the Buddhist gesture of reassurance. A gilded plaster garment was draped over this stone figure at one time, but it, too, is now missing. This area is now bleak and untraveled. But once it was on the main caravan route from India to Russia.

The Kabul museum, in the capital, has a collection of stone heads, ivories, and paintings from early Buddhist sites and from the old mosques.

Afghanistan is a constitutional monarchy, ruled by a king who lives at Kabul. The University of Kabul, and other colleges there, have fine libraries. There is also a good public library. The modern buildings in Kabul are a rare sight in this country where most of the people live as they have for hundreds of years.

Afghan family life is similar to most tribal family life in other Moslem countries. The oldest male has complete authority over every family member. Sons bring their wives home to live in their father's house.

In non-nomad tribes, the family lives in a house or group of houses within a walled area. Each family has a room, or a house, in the family group. These flat-roofed houses usually are one story high, and they all face the common center area.

English Electric Company for World Bank

In the country, some of these family houses are like small forts. They have a tower at each corner from which the countryside can be watched.

Nomads live in dome-shaped *yurts*, which are felt-covered tents. Each yurt is usually big enough for one family. But the family is still part of the larger family group. An encampment may have many yurts in it. The southern nomads use larger tents, often big enough to include all members of the larger family unit.

Although both Afghanistan and Iran are Moslem countries, they have had serious disputes over the use of the water of the Helmand River. This river rises in Afghanistan and flows west and south into Iran.

Pakistan is a divided country. West Pakistan and East Pakistan are about a thousand miles apart. Except for the fact that both parts of Pakistan are Moslem, the two parts of Pakistan are very different from each other.

East Pakistan is a lush, tropical land. Most of it is on the delta where the Ganges (gan'jeez) and the Brahmaputra (brahm-ah-poo'trah) rivers spread out into countless streams and tidal creeks as they flow to the Bay of Bengal. This is marshland, dense with forests of mangrove and home to elephants, tigers, leopards. Monsoons sweep in from the bay bringing heavy rainfall.

Most of the people of East Pakistan are farmers. They raise rice, tea, jute, sugar cane, and palm trees. In the drier sections of the country the farmers live in villages. The houses are made of mud bricks with thatched roofs. In the areas of the heavy rainfall, bamboo houses are built on stilts.

West Pakistan rises in the north to the lofty Himalayas (him-ah-lay'ahz) and the Hindu Kush. The south and west are barren, dry, desert-like areas. In the south the country reaches the Arabian Sea. Though the Indus River and all its tributaries bring some water to this dry land, eighty per cent of the land has to be irrigated. Even the early civilizations in the valleys had irrigation systems. Today new dams are being built.

There are remains of prehistoric civilization in the Indus Valley. There are old Buddhist statues and art objects from the time that the Moguls swept down through Khyber Pass into the valley.

United Nations

Farmers in West Pakistan raise wheat, cotton, sugar cane, and tobacco. Most of the people live by farming. But the new dams are beginning to supply power for industry.

Karachi, on the Arabian Sea, is an important seaport and air terminal. Karachi was the capital of Pakistan until 1962. At that time the national capital was moved to the new city of Islamabad, near Peshwar in the north. The legislative capital is in Dacca in East Pakistan. Unusual in a Moslem nation, six seats are reserved for women.

Pakistan was created when the British left India in 1947. It is a member of the British Commonwealth of Nations. Before 1947, Pakistan was part of India.

As soon as independence was declared, religious riots broke out in both India and Pakistan. Hindu refugees fled from Pakistan to India and Moslem refugees fled from India to Pakistan. Many of these people left areas where their families had lived for hundreds of years.

below: Two young girls walking on sewer pipes in Dacca, East Pakistan

Land of Hindus and Buddhists

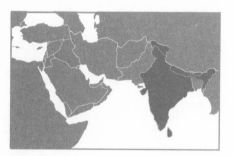

India, like a giant triangle, drops its point into the Indian Ocean. The Arabian Sea is on its west side. The Bay of Bengal on its east.

If you come into India in the north—which is unlikely—you will find you are in the Himalaya Mountains. Their snow-capped peaks reach 20,000 feet into the air.

These cold, inhospitable peaks fall away toward the south through wooded foothills. Here you will find cattle grazing and tea growing on the slopes of the fertile valleys.

Rivers rising in the mountains have brought silt to build up broad and fertile plains. The Ganges River basin is about 1,500 miles long and as much as four hundred miles wide in some places. This is densely settled farmland, where sometimes several crops are grown in one season.

Most of the main peninsula of India is a plateau, cut off from the river basin country by the Vindhya Mountains. Along the sea to the east and the west, low mountains called the Ghats drop to the lowland of the coast. There is some farming on the plateau, but much of it is rugged forest land, home of primitive tribes.

Forest, swamps, and jungles are home to many wild animals including tigers, elephants, and leopards. The cobra and other poisonous snakes are found here, too.

Elephants are tamed and put to work. An injured tiger may turn man-eater and pick off a worker on a tea plantation.

India is a land of rare beauty like that found in the Vale of Kashmir (cash'meer). It is a land of contrasts. Here are some of the most beautiful buildings in the world, and also villages of mud huts. Millions of cows, sacred to the Hindus, wander among the hungry people. India has a long history of culture, art, and literature, but many of the people cannot read or write. One of the problems of education is that there are so many languages. Fourteen languages are official, and there are more than two hundred that are not official!

There are almost 450 million people in India, and eighty-five per cent of them are Hindus. The government is encouraging the use of Hindi as a national language, but millions of people do not speak it. To advance in government or business, Indians must be able to read and write both Hindi and English.

Although the Moslems ruled India for about 500 years, most of the people remained Hindu. The British ruled India for 300 years. Then, due for the most part to the quiet work of Mahandes (Mahatma) Gandhi, India won its independence in 1947. This was when Pakistan became a separate country.

Everywhere you look in India you see women wearing the graceful sari, a ten-yard length of cloth with one end wound around the body and the other thrown over the left shoulder. The best saris are of silk; less expensive ones are cotton. You see women working in the fields and homes with their saris wrapped tightly around them.

below: Young Indian boys

For centuries, the Indians have been skillful hand-weavers, weaving the cloth for the saris and for the brightly colored turbans worn by so many of the men. The finest silk for saris has the pattern woven into it. Cotton for saris is usually woven plain, and the design is then printed on the cloth with small, wooden, handcarved blocks. Today we call brightly printed cotton cloth calico, after Calcutta, a large city on the Bay of Bengal. The poorer Indians wear clothes of a coarse cotton fabric called *dungri* in Hindi. This is where our word dungarees comes from.

Indian art seems to be mainly sculpture. Everywhere you look there are statues of Siva, Vishnu, and Brahma, the trinity of the Hindu religion. There are many lesser gods. Each has many sides to his character, and these are worshipped at different festivals and by different groups.

To Hindus, the Ganges River is the holiest river in India. People who live near the river come down to it to bathe every morning. (A Hindu must bathe before he says his morning prayers.) Those who live farther away try to get to the Ganges at least once, to bathe away their sins in the sacred river.

Varanasi, formerly Benares, on the Ganges is the holiest city in the world for Hindus. The name of this 3000-year-old city means "salvation place," and Hindus believe that if you die near this city, or on the left bank of the Ganges, you will enter heaven immediately and not be reborn many times.

Allahabad is at the junction of the Ganges and the Juma rivers. The *Magh Mela,* a Hindu religious festival, is celebrated here every spring. Thousands of holy men come to bathe in the rivers. Every twelve years a special festival, the *Kumbh Mela,* is held. All Hindus try to come to Alla-habad at that time. The crowds are so great that people are sometimes crushed to death.

Even more than most Asian countries, India reflects the past. It is only in this ancient, colorful land that people still worship in a temple 4000 years old.

One of the most famous and beautiful buildings in the world is the Taj Mahal at Agra. This lovely building is a

above left: A woman wears a variation of the Indian sari

An Indian snake charmer with his king cobra in New Delhi

tomb. It was built by Shah Jahan, a Moslem emperor, in memory of his favorite wife. The building was begun in 1631 and finished seventeen years later.

The West Gate, as you come through it, is a hundred feet high. The lettering on the gate is so well-proportioned that the letters at the top appear to be the same size as those at the base. Step through the gate and you see the building set in the garden that surrounds it. The walk leading to the terrace on which the Taj Mahal is built is lined with cypress trees. And the building is reflected in the pools of water in front of it. The inside walls are covered with mosaics made of jewels. The room in which Shah Jahan and his "Elite of the Palace" are buried has walls of delicately carved lattice work.

Twenty-three miles from Agra is Fatehpur, the "City of Victory." It was built in 1570 by the Moslem emperor Akbar. Lack of water made the builders abandon the city fifty years after it was completed. Among the most interesting places here is the Parchesi Court. This is laid out like a checker board with brightly colored squares. Women of the royal harem were the living chess pieces for games played on this board!

New Delhi, the capital of India, is a new city. The government buildings were built by the British and were first used in 1931. The buildings were turned over to the Indian government when India became independent in 1947.

In New Delhi there is a modern shrine, as important to the people of India as any religious temple. This is the *Raj Ghat*, the place where Mahatma Gandhi was cremated in 1948. Gandhi's Garden Memorial is nearby. Here is where he fell when he was shot.

The new capital of Punjab, Chandigarh, is almost all new. The buildings were designed by the modern French master architect, Le Corbusier. Although the buildings are strikingly modern, Le Corbusier has captured Indian style without copying Indian architecture.

opposite top: Cargo boats at Aleppey, Kerala, India. This city is called the "Venice of the East" because of its river setting.

opposite bottom: Indian workers carry coconut palm leaves that will be used to make thatched roofs

Calcutta, capital of Bengal, is at the head of the Bay of Bengal. It is a bustling industrial city. There are iron and steel mills, tanneries, and jute mills. Calcutta was the capital of India during much of the British rule.

Bombay, on the west coast, is built on what used to be seven small islands. This is a large, important seaport and industrial center where there are many museums. Many leading citizens of Bombay are members of an ancient Persian religious sect who settled in India 2000 years ago.

Ceylon is an island off the southern tip of India. It looks as if a chip had been broken off the point of the Indian triangle and set adrift in the Indian Ocean.

Ceylon is an independent nation and part of the British Commonwealth. Most of the land is flat, but there are mountains in the south and west. Ceylon is close to the equator so the climate varies very little, except that it is cooler in the mountains.

Most of the people are Singhalese, a native Buddhist group. There are also Tamils. Most of them are Hindus and came to Ceylon from southern India. Descendants of the Tamils who came to Ceylon five or six hundred years ago are considered Ceylonese. However, the Tamils who came within the last hundred years to work in the large plantations are considered "Indian" by the Ceylon government. The government of India considers them Ceylonese. They have no citizenship rights in either country.

More than half the people in Ceylon work on the tea, rubber, and coconut plantations. Ceylon grows a large amount of rice, but only half enough for the needs of the people. The rest must be imported.

Columbo, the capital, is an important seaport and much cleaner than most Asian cities. Women wear the colorful sari and beautiful jewels. Most men wear western suits, although a few still wear the native *sarong*, a long skirt wrapped tightly around the body.

The ancient cities of Anuradhapura and Polonnaruwa were capitals of Ceylon in ancient times.

opposite: An elephant in Ceylon moves a palm tree log

opposite top: Fishing boats in the harbor at Colombo, Ceylon

opposite bottom: A ''toddy-tapper'' walks from palm tree to palm tree checking the crop in Colombo, Ceylon

left: A Moslem mosque in Colombo, Ceylon

Trans World Airlines Photo

The oldest tree in the world is in Anuradhapura. It is a 2,300-year-old Bo-tree, grown from a branch of the tree in Buddh Gaya, India, under which Buddha meditated. The branch was brought to Ceylon by Princess Sanghamitta, daughter of Asoka, the great Indian ruler in the third century B.C.

Nepal is a small, narrow country lying between the curve of northern India and Tibet. It is a constitutional monarchy.

Three mountain ranges, including the Himalayas, cross this little country from east to west. The plains in the south are an extension of the Indian plains. On the border of Tibet, Mount Everest rises 29,028 feet high. It is the tallest mountain in the world. The top of Everest was reached for the first time in 1953 by Edmund Hillary of New Zealand, and Tenzing, a Sherpa guide. The Sherpas are a hardy tribe that live high in the mountains, farming a little and raising yaks. They know the mountains and are often hired as porters and guides by climbers.

Before Everest was climbed in 1949 no foreigners were allowed in the country, except mountain climbers. Even they often had trouble getting permits. Since Everest was climbed, however, the outside world has shown much interest in Nepal and the policy has been changed.

The royal family are descendants of the king of Gurkha. Gurkha was a small country near Tibet before 1769 when its ruler conquered the rest of what is Nepal. The famous soldiers of Nepal, called Gurkas, are drawn from some of the tribes who lived in the small kingdom of Gurkha. Fierce fighters, these men are still native soldiers in the British army.

Nepal is filled with shrines and temples. There are more than 2,700 of them in Katmandu Valley alone. The royal

A fishing crew hauls in the catch from the Indian Ocean

family is Hindu, but there are many Buddhists in the country. The Buddhist monasteries are quite poor. Butter is burned in altar lamps in these temples, and prayer wheels and banners are in motion everywhere throughout the land.

Most of the people are farmers. In Katmandu Valley, most houses are made of stone or mud bricks and have thatched roofs. In the southern plains, houses are often made of bamboo. They have two rooms, one for cooking and one for sleeping. The Sherpas, living high in the mountains, build houses of stone and wood, roofed with boards.

Sikkim is a tiny country just east of Nepal. It is a protectorate of India, ruled by a native king and his queen, a young American girl.

There are about 160,000 people in this mountainous little country. Most of them are farmers who grow rice, millet, and vegetables. The spice cardamon is grown for export.

Like other Buddhists, their lives are governed by ritual.

Bhutan is east of Sikkim and bigger. It is another mountainous country, but here the mountains run north and south. In the foothills near the Indian plains, rainfall averages between 200 and 250 inches a year. Bhutan is often called "Land of the Thunder Dragon," because of its frequent and violent thunderstorms.

There is very little level space for farming. Most of the fields are terraced. Water for irrigation is brought to the fields in stone aqueducts. Some timber is exported.

The people live in houses made of stone put together with clay. Or they are made of clay mixed with small stones. The houses are two to four stories high, connected with ladders instead of staircases. Sliding shutters keep out the cold and the roofs are pitched sharply so that snow will slide off.

The only foreigners allowed into Bhutan are those who have been invited by the king.

We have come a long way since disembarking at Jiddah in Saudi Arabia. We have traveled through lands older than history and we have seen new countries groping their way to responsible places in the family of independent nations. Uneasy peace within many of these countries, and along their borders, keeps them in the news as history continues to be made.

INDEX: Young People's Story of Africa and Asia

Type	*Century Expanded*
Typesetter	*American Typesetting Corporation*
Printer	*The Regensteiner Corporation*